All About Cheetahs

MW01245456

By: Reid Coleman

Introduction

Do you like cheetahs? If you do, then you are in luck. This book contains all kinds of awesome information about cheetahs. Dive in and enjoy!

How Fast?

Cheetahs are very fast. They can go up to 75 mph! They can accelerate to that speed in about 3 seconds!! They are also the fastest land animals on the planet.

A Cheetahs Prey

Cheetahs eat small to medium-size animals like hares, impalas, wildebeest calves, and gazelles. Most of these animals are hard to catch because they are also very fast, almost as fast as a cheetah, but not quite!

Cheetahs Teeth

Cheetahs are carnivores. They have long teeth and sharp molars that are great for cutting through meat and bone.

Female Cheetahs

While the male cheetah is hunting for food, the female usually stays home with the cubs and protects them from other animals that could be a threat. The female cheetah cares for the cubs until age 3, when they are considered full grown.

Male Cheetahs

Male Cheetahs are usually responsible for hunting. They are slightly larger than females, and also have bigger heads. They are also typically faster by about 5 mph, and protect the territory that they live in.

Cubs

Cheetah cubs are very cute and tiny. They are blind when they are born, but as they get older week by week, they open their eyes and start running and playing. It is not until they are about 2 years old, when they are considered full grown hunters.

Habitat

Cheetahs live and hunt in Africa and small parts Iran. They prefer to live in grasslands as they blend in well with the environment and there are a wide variety of prey that cheetahs like to eat.

The King Cheetah

The king Cheetah is a mix between a Cheetah and a leopard. Unlike a normal Cheetah, the king Cheetah has stripes and spots instead of just spots. King Cheetahs are very rare animals, so it is less likely that two King Cheetahs will find each other to mate. This limits their population.

Cheetahs in the Wild

Cheetahs in the wild are dying and it is up to us to protect them! on the next page is a list of things that you can do to protect Cheetahs in the wild.

How to Protect Cheetahs

1. Respect wildlife.

2. Make a donation to protect Cheetah habitats.

3. Spread the word on how to protect Cheetahs!

5 Fast Facts

1. Cheetahs usually hunt alone

2. Cheetahs are the fastest land animal

3. Cheetahs can weigh 75-145 pounds

4. Cheetahs can run up to 75 mph

5. Cheetahs do not roar they meow!

About the Author

Reid is 9 years old and likes playing with his dog Henry, riding his hover board and playing outside.

Cool Cheetah Photos!

Cool Cheetah Photos!

Cool Cheetah Photos!

Cool Cheetah Photos!

Cool Cheetah Photos!

Cool Cheetah Photos!

Cool Cheetah Photos!

Cool Cheetah Photos!

Cool Cheetah Photos!

CPSIA information can be obtained
at www.ICGtesting.com
Printed in the USA
BVHW061451110722
641846BV00013B/241